It's R!

Katherine Hengel

Consulting Editor, Diane Craig, M.A./Reading Specialist

ABDO
Publishing Company

Published by ABDO Publishing Company, 8000 West 78th Street, Edina, Minnesota 55439. Copyright © 2010 by Abdo Consulting Group, Inc. International copyrights reserved in all countries. No part of this book may be reproduced in any form without written permission from the publisher. Super SandCastle™ is a trademark and logo of ABDO Publishing Company.

Printed in the United States.

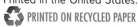 PRINTED ON RECYCLED PAPER

Editor: Liz Salzmann
Content Developer: Nancy Tuminelly
Cover and Interior Design and Production: Kelly Doudna, Mighty Media
Photo Credits: iStockphoto (Nathan Blaney, Jani Bryson), Shutterstock

Library of Congress Cataloging-in-Publication Data
Hengel, Katherine.
  It's R! / Katherine Hengel.
    p. cm. -- (It's the alphabet!)
  ISBN 978-1-60453-605-8
  1. English language--Alphabet--Juvenile literature. 2. Alphabet books--Juvenile literature. I. Title.
  PE1155.H4683 2010
  421'.1--dc22
  〈E〉
                        2009022028

Super SandCastle™ books are created by a team of professional educators, reading specialists, and content developers around five essential components— phonemic awareness, phonics, vocabulary, text comprehension, and fluency—to assist young readers as they develop reading skills and strategies and increase their general knowledge. All books are written, reviewed, and leveled for guided reading, early reading intervention, and Accelerated Reader® programs for use in shared, guided, and independent reading and writing activities to support a balanced approach to literacy instruction.

About SUPER SANDCASTLE™

Bigger Books for Emerging Readers
Grades K–4

Created for library, classroom, and at-home use, Super SandCastle™ books support and engage young readers as they develop and build literacy skills and will increase their general knowledge about the world around them. Super SandCastle™ books are an extension of SandCastle™, the leading preK–3 imprint for emerging and beginning readers. Super SandCastle™ features a larger trim size for more reading fun.

Let Us Know
Super SandCastle™ would like to hear your stories about reading this book. What was your favorite page? Was there something hard that you needed help with? Share the ups and downs of learning to read. We want to hear from you! Send us an e-mail.

sandcastle@abdopublishing.com

Contact us for a complete list of SandCastle™, Super SandCastle™, and other nonfiction and fiction titles from ABDO Publishing Company.

www.abdopublishing.com • 8000 West 78th Street
Edina, MN 55439 • 800-800-1312 • 952-831-1632 fax

Aa Bb Cc Dd Ee

Ff Gg Hh Ii Jj Kk

Ll Mm Nn Oo Pp

Qq Rr Ss Tt Uu Vv

Ww Xx Yy Zz

The Letter

Rr

The letter r in American Sign Language

R and r can also look like

Rr **Rr**

Rr Rr

Rr Rr

The letter **r** is a consonant.

It is the 18th letter of the alphabet.

Some words start with **r**.

raccoon

rock

6

The letter r always makes the same sound.

river

R

The raccoon rests on a round, red rock by the river.

Some words have **r** in the middle.

turtle

turkey

8

Brandon

Before breakfast Brandon draws a picture of a turkey and a turtle in a forest.

Some words have **r** at the end.

chair

flower

10

mother

Jennifer

Jennifer sits in a chair and her mother puts a flower in her hair near her ear.

Some words have a double **r**.

blueberries

carrots

Derrick carries carrots and blueberries in a barrel.

barrel

wren

wreath

Lawrence writes about a wren that wrecks a wreath with a wrench.

wrench

14

Ruby loves the great outdoors and breathing clean, fresh air.

She cares about the earth and is proud of her red hair.

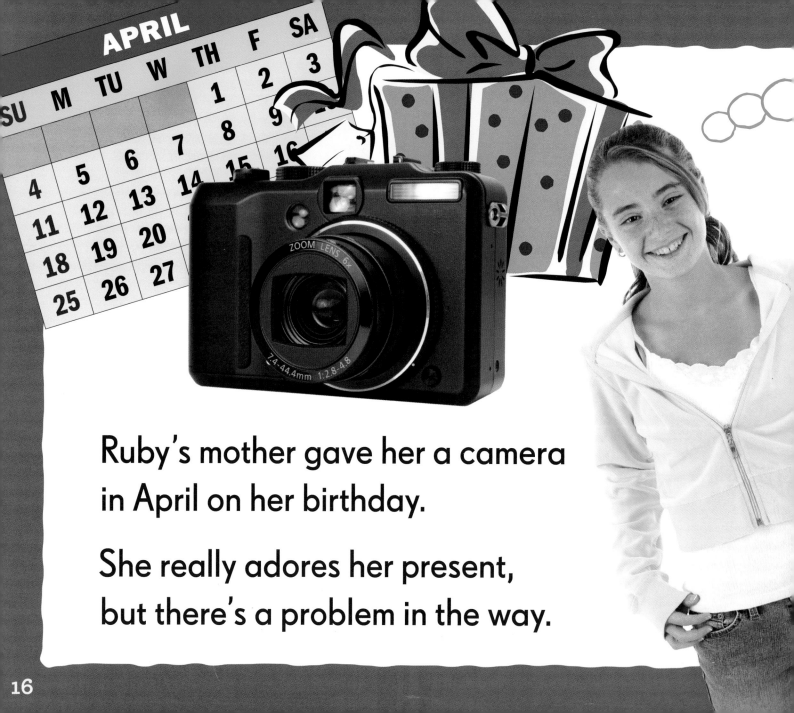

Ruby's mother gave her a camera in April on her birthday.

She really adores her present, but there's a problem in the way.

Ruby dreams of taking pictures of forests, rocks, and more.

However Ruby has never tried to use a camera before!

Then Ruby remembers her favorite aunt takes pictures of her dog Rover.

She writes a letter that says,
"Aunt Rebecca, please hurry over!"

Ruby learns about her camera
from Aunt Rebecca, who is never wrong.

They drive to the river together
and take pictures all day long.

Now Ruby carries her camera everywhere, shooting robins, wrens, and trees.

But don't ever try to take Ruby's picture, not even if you say please!

Which words have
the letter **r**?

robin

rock

raccoon

cake

ball

tree

chair

pickle

23

Glossary

adore (p. 16) – to like very much.

barrel (p. 12) – a large, round container, usually made of wood or metal.

fresh (p. 15) – clean and natural.

great outdoors (p. 15) – nature or wilderness.

proud (p. 15) – pleased or satisfied about something you have or did.

really (p. 16) – very or very much.

shoot (p. 20) – to take a picture of something with a camera.

wreath (p. 13) – a circle made of flowers or branches twisted together.

wreck (p. 13) – to destroy.

wren (pp. 13, 20) – a small, brown songbird.

wrench (p. 13) – a tool used to hold or turn something.

To promote letter recognition, letters are highlighted instead of glossary words in this series. The page numbers above indicate where the glossary words can be found.

More Words with **R**

Find the **r** in the beginning, middle, or end of each word.

barn	fire	rabbit	ride	room
circle	girl	ram	right	row
color	kangaroo	rat	rip	rule
deer	large	read	road	under
every	number	rent	rob	very
father	paper	rich	robot	were